VEHICLES OF GODS

Indra and Airavat the Elephant

Shubha Vilas

Om KIDZ
An imprint of Om Books International

Brahma had granted Indra a special elephant as his escort. Airavat was not an ordinary elephant. He was the king of all elephants. His snowy-white skin made him look divine. His four tusks and seven trunks made him something special. He was a king fit only for a king. He rightly deserved to be the escort of Indradeva, the king of heavens.

Despite everything, Airavat was feeling guilty and ashamed. So ashamed, that he was hiding at the bottom of the ocean. He could not bear to show his face to anyone. He was thankful that no one could see his tears as they flowed out of his heart into the ocean.

He alone was responsible for the pitiable condition of all devatas. As the memory of that event came rushing back into his mind, he shuddered and trembled. As much as he tried, he could not forget that day.

It was a lovely day in Indraloka. Airavat was busy supervising the heavy security at the gate. Durvasa Muni had just gone in to meet Lord Indra.

The Muni happily gave his garland to Indra as a token of love. Indra accepted the garland and passed it on to Airavat, who happened to be standing beside him.

Airavat held the garland on his trunk, not sure what to do with it. So he flung it on the ground and merrily trampled it.

When he was done with it, he realised there was an eerie silence. He looked up to see the shocked faces of Durvasa Muni and Indradeva. To his horror, they were both looking at him in anger. Airavat shrunk back in fear.

'You dare to disrespect the garland I gave?' Durvasa Muni's face was red with anger. Indra had turned pale. He knew that Durvasa would inflict on him a terrible curse. Airavat was too stunned to even move.

Durvasa Muni turned towards Indra and threw a curse upon all the devatas. 'Because devatas are too proud of their eternal youth, I curse each and every devata to lose their youth and start aging.'

In an instant, Indra was at the sage's feet, begging him to take back the curse. Indra's humility and sorrow jolted the sage back to reality and he felt a wave of sympathy for him. 'The only way now to stop you from aging is to drink the nectar from the ocean,' he said.

Durvasa Muni then sped away. The devatas were shell-shocked! As the days passed, the devatas began to suffer the signs of old age like wrinkles, loss of eyesight and weak bones.

At last, the devatas and demons began churning the ocean for the celestial nectar. They wanted to become young again.

Many precious treasures came out of the ocean during the churning. Airavat, who had been hiding there, also had to come out.

Indra was overjoyed to have got back his favourite elephant who had gone missing for quite some time. Airavat was very pleased to learn that he had been forgiven. And once the devatas drank the nectar, they got back their eternal youth. Airavat was happy once again.